WHO MADE THESE TRACKS?

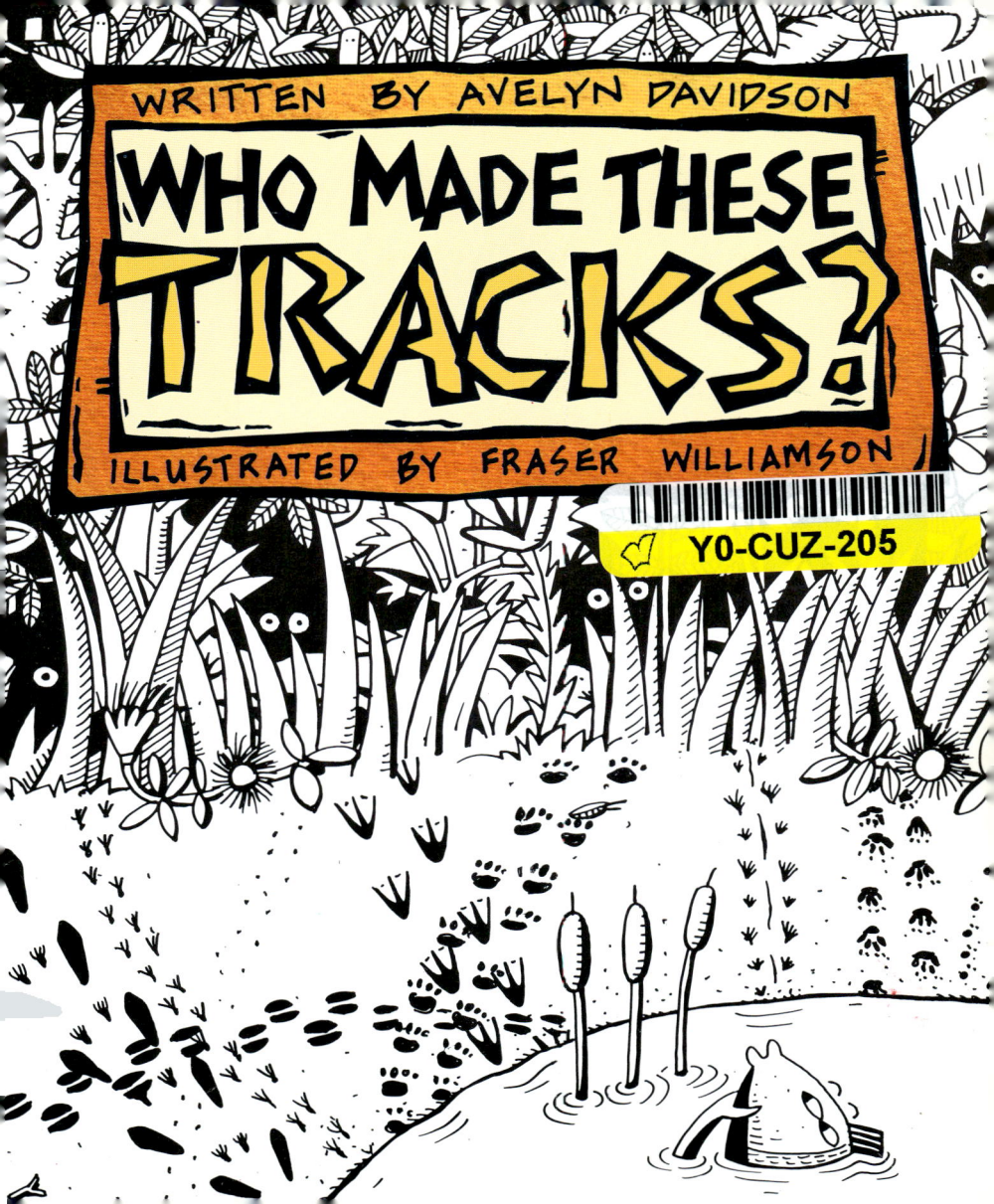

WRITTEN BY AVELYN DAVIDSON

ILLUSTRATED BY FRASER WILLIAMSON

Who made these tracks?

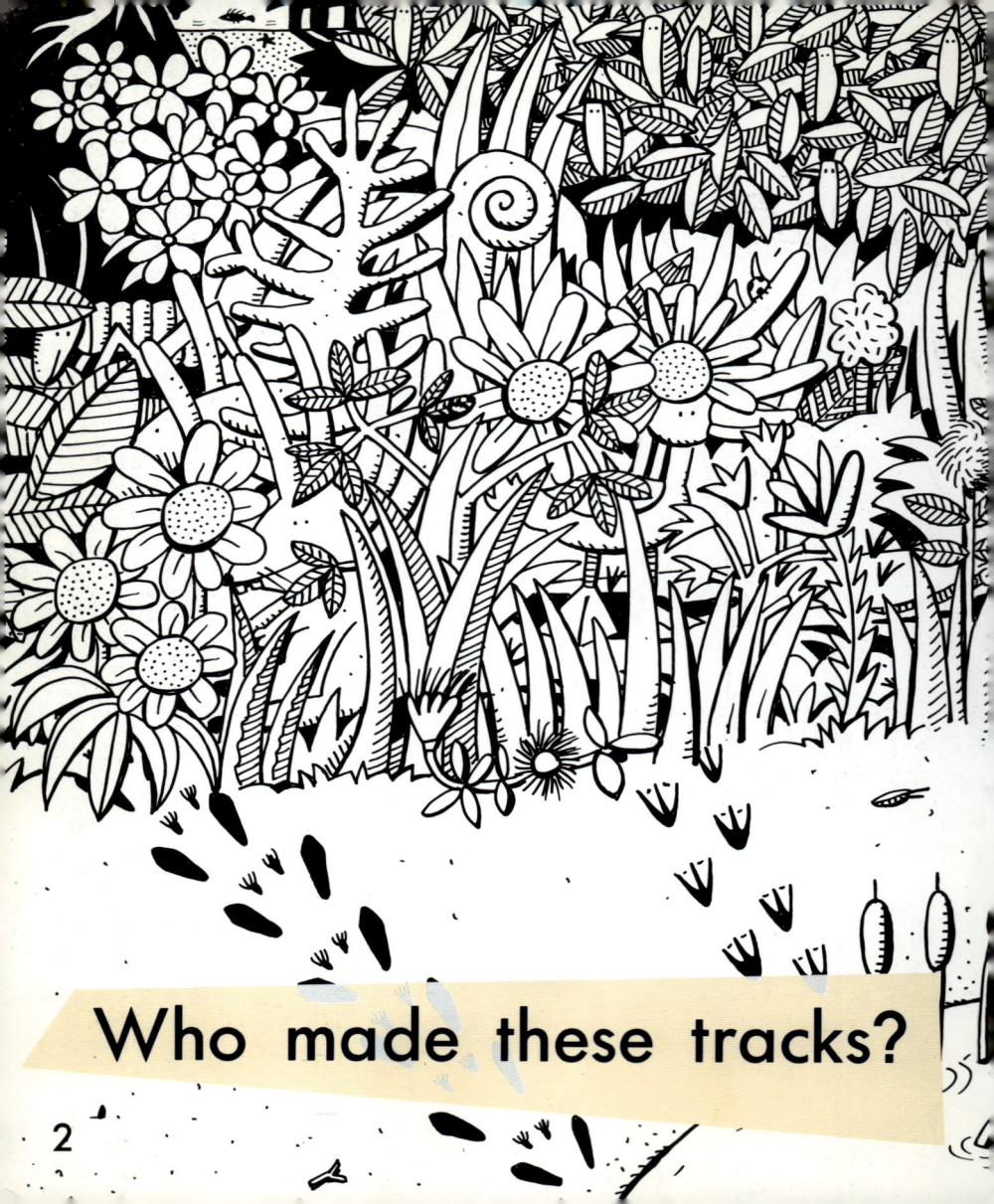

3

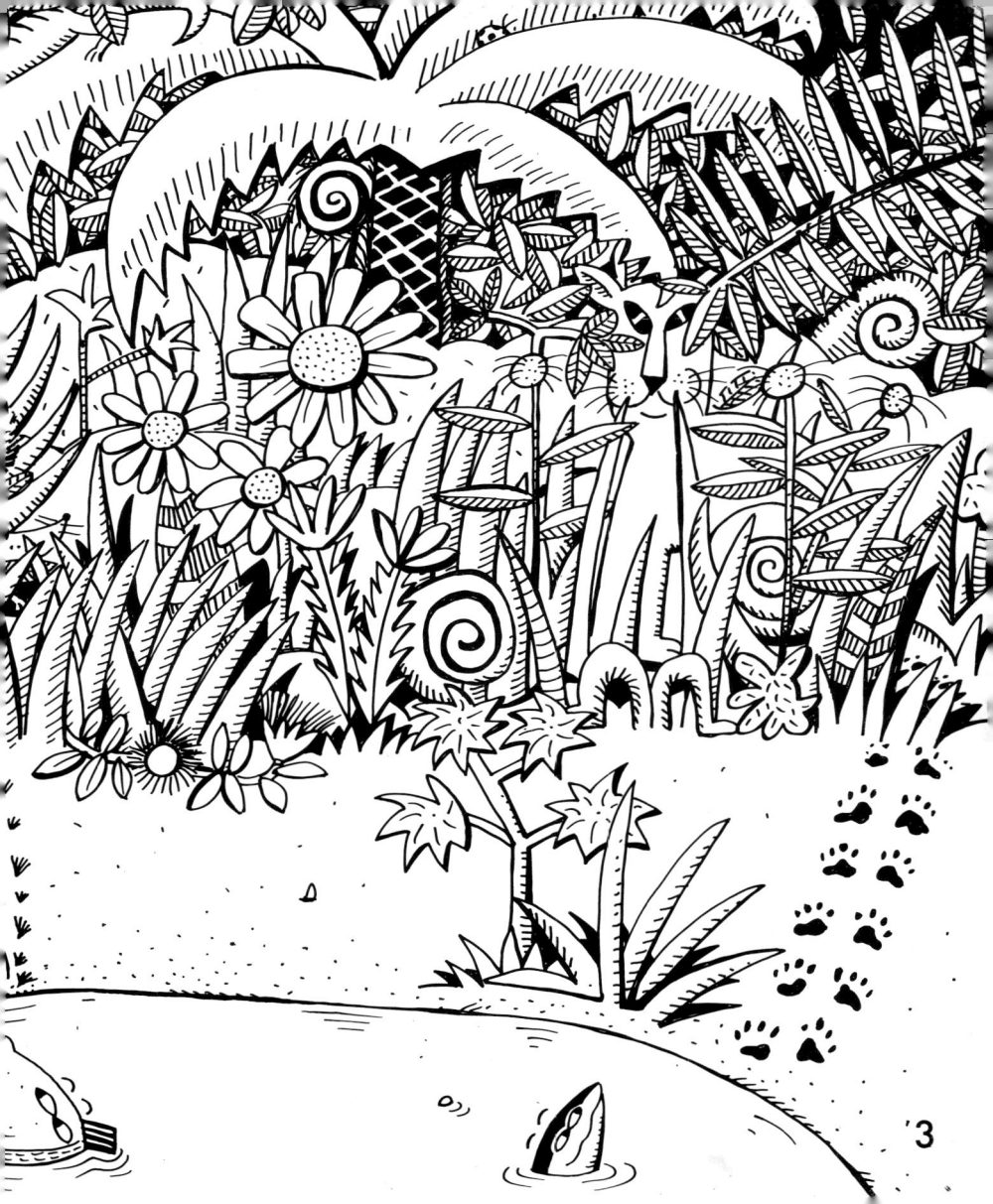

Rabbit made these tracks.

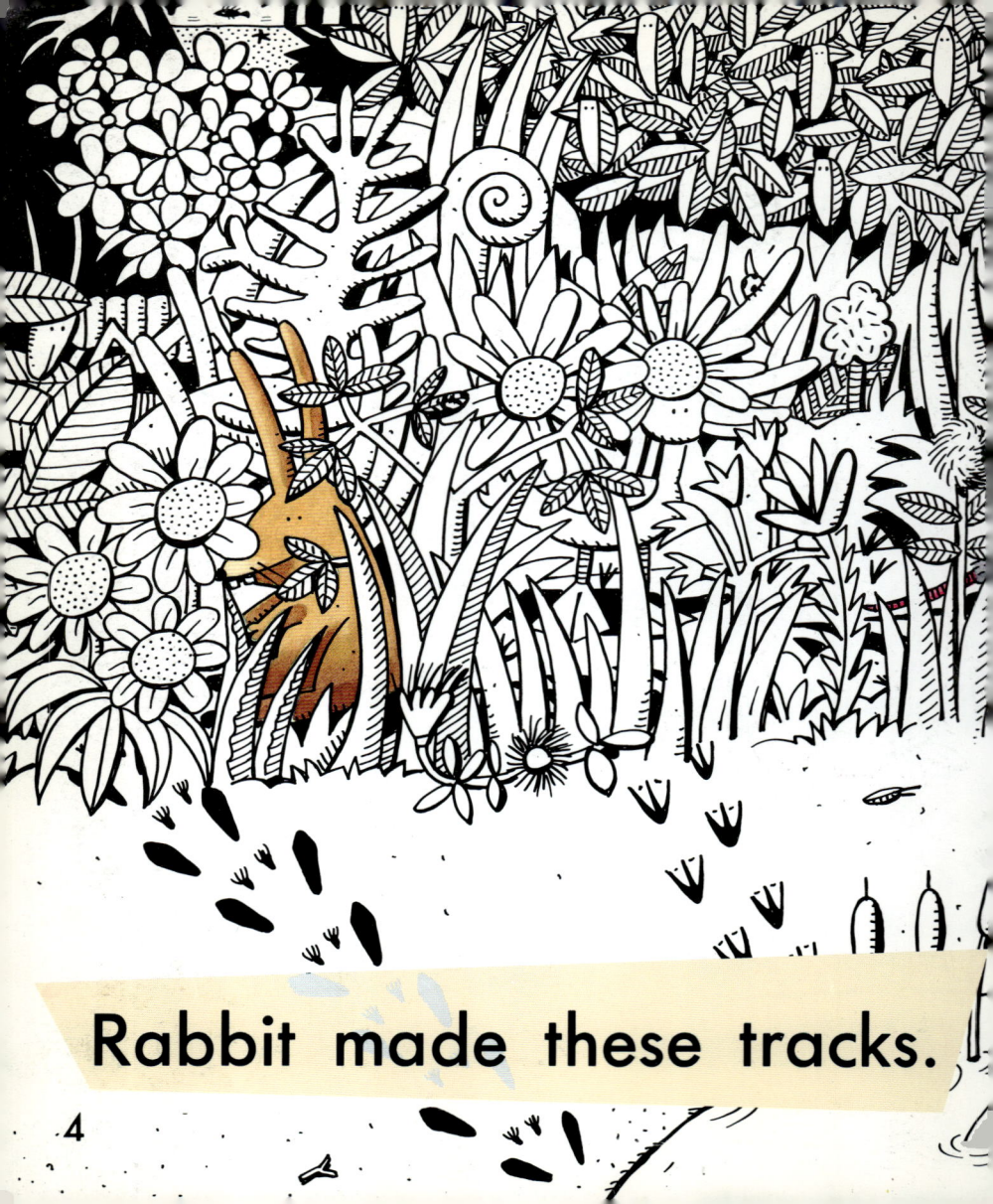

4

Mouse made these tracks.

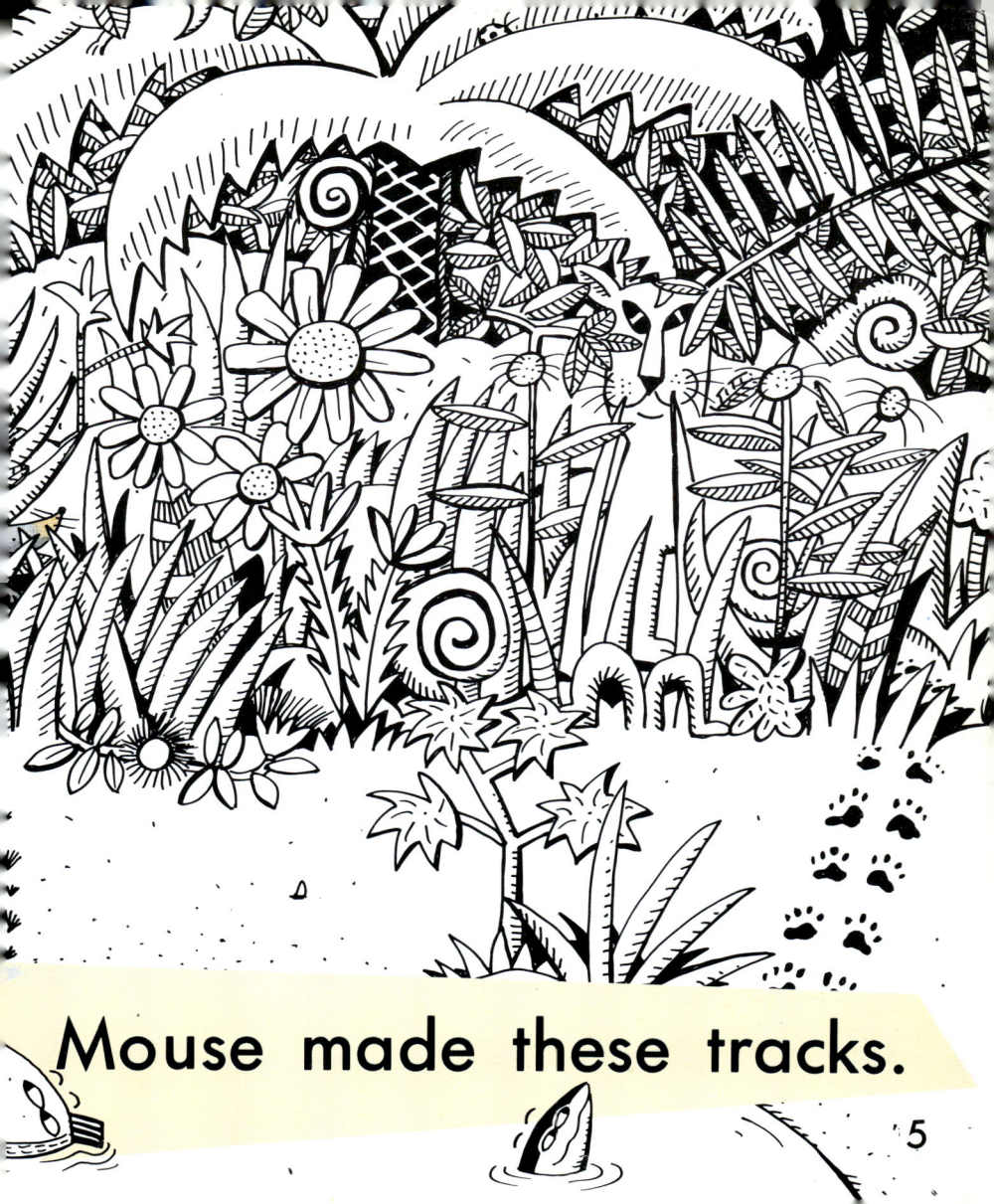

5

Duck made these tracks.

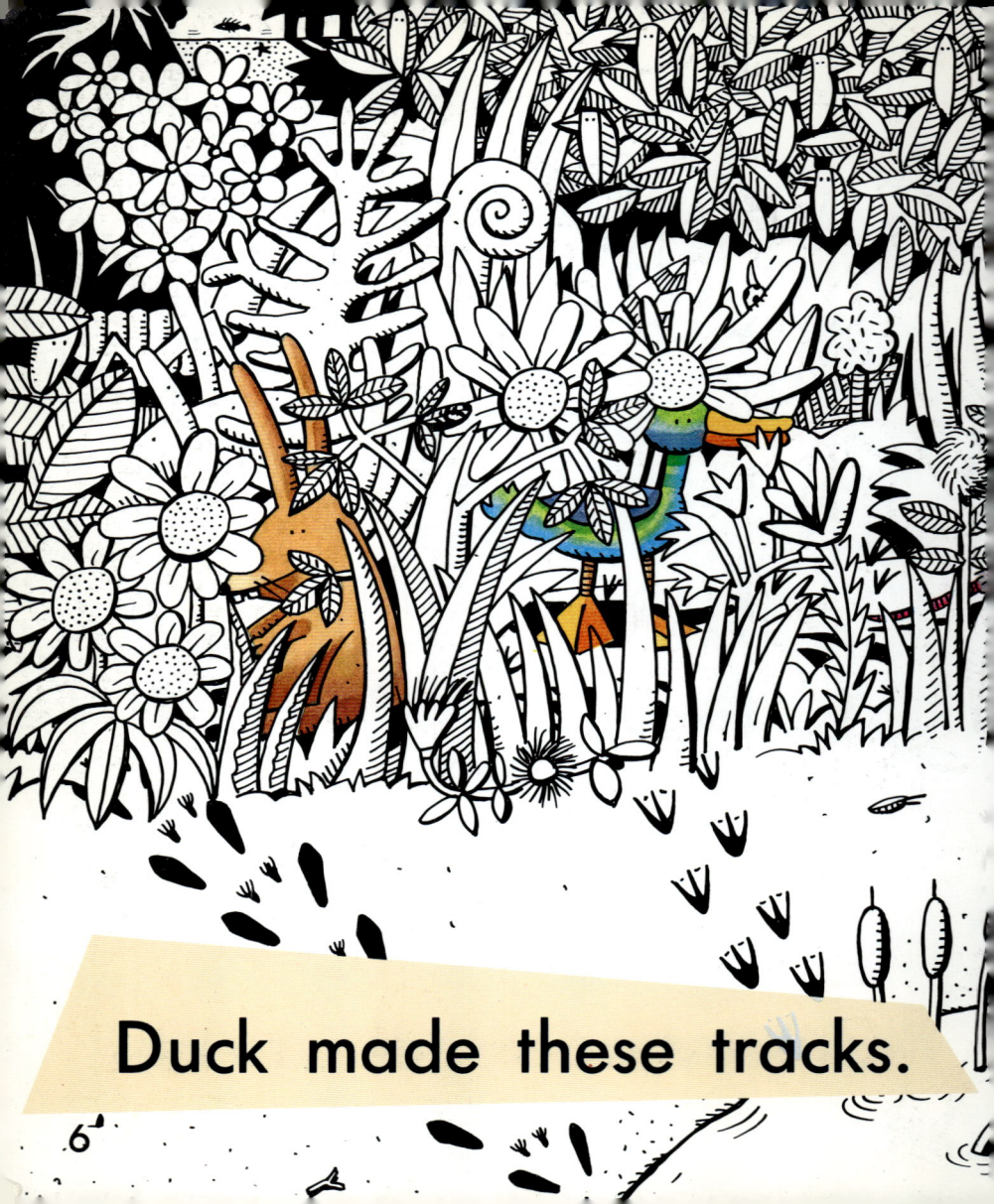

6

Cat made these tracks.

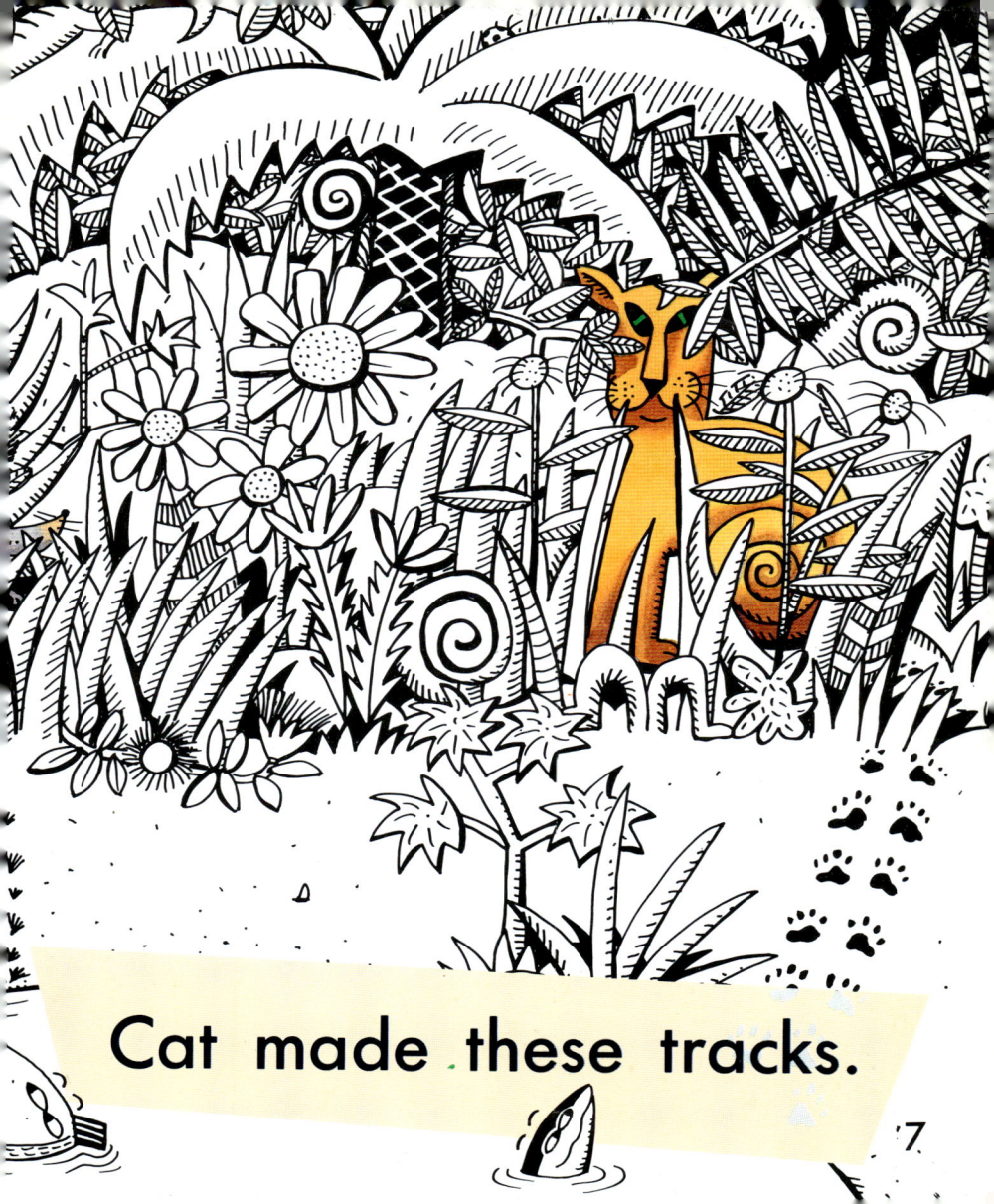

Who made these tracks?

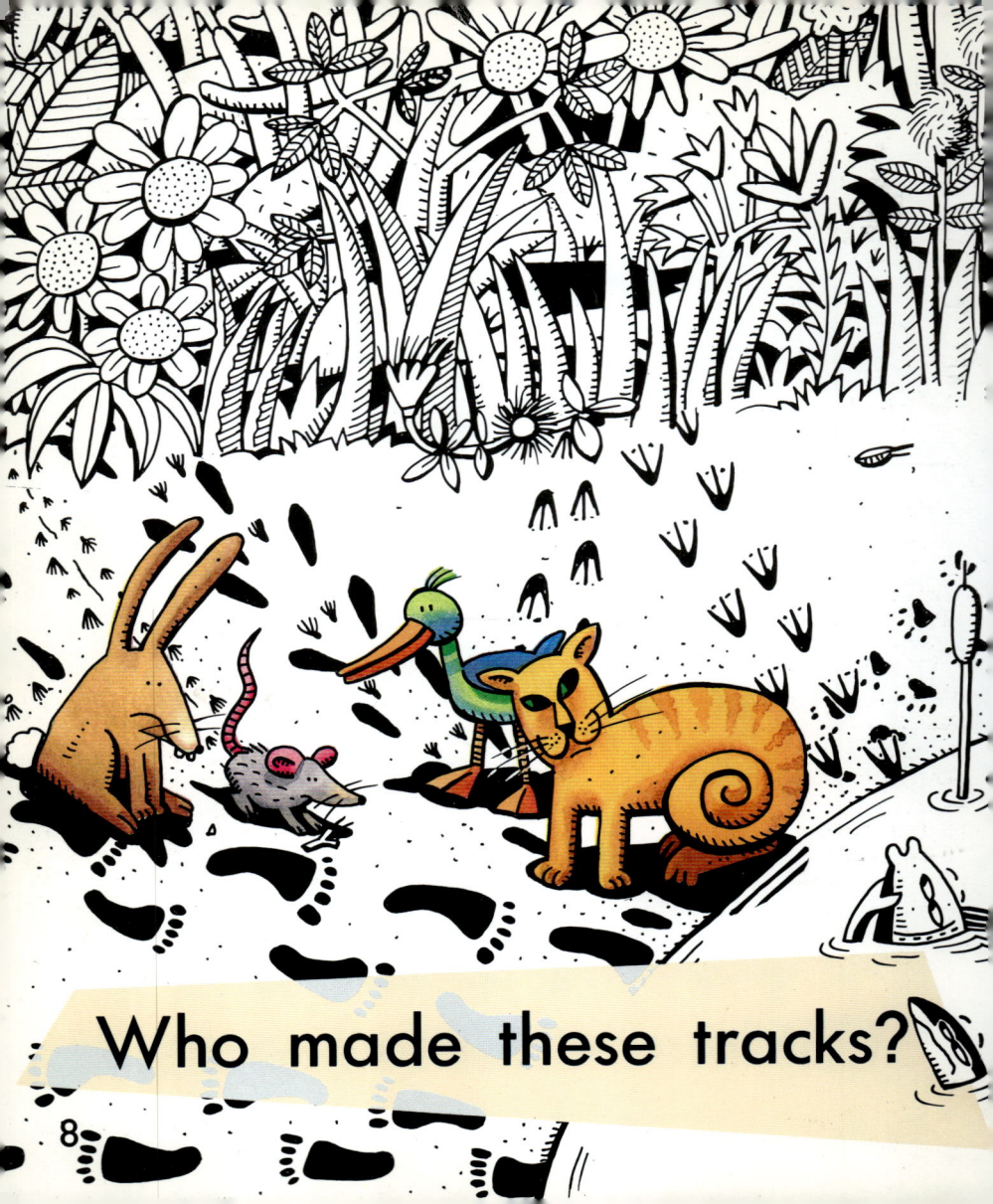